Atopia

MW00424101

Wesleyan Poetry

PIA

SANDRA SIMONDS

WESLEYAN UNIVERSITY PRESS Middletown, Connecticut

Wesleyan University Press
Middletown CT 06459
www.wesleyan.edu/wespress
2019 © Sandra Simonds
All rights reserved
Manufactured in the United States of America
Designed by Richard Hendel
Typeset in Monotype Walbaum

Library of Congress Cataloging-in-Publication Data
available upon request

Hardcover ISBN: 978-0-8195-7919-5
Paperback ISBN: 978-0-8195-7904-1
Ebook ISBN: 978-0-8195-7905-8

5 4 3 2 1

CONTENTS

Atopia

When you think about it, mostly, a cage is air—
So what is there
to be afraid of?
A cage of air. Baudelaire said
Poe thought America was one giant cage.
To the poet, a nation is one big cage.
And isn't the nation mostly filled with air?
Try to put a cage around your dream.
The cage escapes the dream.
I see it streak and stream.

Night is the insane asylum of plants—Raúl Zurita

Everyone dreams of the apocalypse, they are barfing
into their grief but I, love, dream of you, and I am old enough
to know this is not the apocalypse, and I am well-read
enough to know all of this was set in motion long
ago, plummet of seashells, the visions loud,
obnoxious even, yes, I try to ignore them, but to no avail,
the dead workers stream through my body, out my finger
tips towards the moon's underlying reality, trumps, keys,
some move into hysteria then collapse or perhaps
this is a vision of souls surrounded by black clouds, layers
of breath, to close one's mind to extraneous events,
life streaming from chambers, music as event and so,
love, I enter the scene before me, as many poets
have before, walk through the gates of the imaginative
space I have to create Dante, Milton, Plath, Lorde,
leave the body, leave the comfort and pain of the body,
enter the inferno, enter on the day of the Oakland
fire when thirty-six lives are lost, one life for each year of mine,
put my head to my knees, whisper, chant, sing, suggest,
rip up the text of my hair, the alephs of my hair,
my long black hair is a text and I will not cut it, my hair
is a parable, a fantasy, a stage, it is burning, turning
to snakes, witches, elves, it is an enormous
Frankenstein on fire and the warehouse went up in its mass,
and the body politic bled down, the dead queers, dead artists,
crisis of landlords and evictions, midwinter, I leave
this body behind, I had to see, I had to see what
was behind the mirror's arrangement of energy
and madness, had to see through this furious parabola.

I am a terrible American
So suicidal
I am a terrible, suicidal American
who throws herself into your desiccated bank vaults
Yet I do not want America to kill me before I kill myself
I can't stand my positive acquisitions
I throw them to the dogs like marrowless bones
I can't stand my drinking
I hate the fires of money
I feel no nationalism
I feel no nationalism in my heart, my hands, my brain, or my pussy
I myself am worse than a rogue state
I feel peeled away from society
I will never leave my bed
I want to die in my bed with the covers over my head
The books I have written for other people sicken me like plague
The books I have written for so little money like a ghost tripping on
    the pavement to get to you
I will be forced out of my enemy's hands like sweaty nickels in the
    wavy grasses
America, I am the moors you lack
My voice crosses you like some bleak financial awareness
I crash like a bombed-out calamity
I am no good for anyone
The vines of my thoughts are the cries of all the people and
    animals you kill
I am the home of the birds and that's all I will ever be
Inside my heart is a boat of Noahs
The animals are cacophonous
I am the town washed away
I starve myself every day

I am the downed power lines of your literature
I spark up from the pavement like the jolting of a corpse
I am that corpse who jolts up and goes on a long walk
America, I am a long walk in your dying wilderness

—※—

I cross the bridge hopeless.
Give me back my dream of the swarm of bears
I cry to the pollution brigade.
"What did the bears do to you?"
"Nothing, my love, they were indifferent."

—※—

I am a black diamond from the asteroid of visions.
Furious, I have splattered my loot into the earth.
The thing is that I look gray
and gray things look half-dead.
The moon is the half-dead body of noon dredged
from those furiously remote acres of myth.

—※—

I wanted resplendent queer sex.
I pulled the hair from my head
like a Greek lament.
My head was a giddy gyre.
No one could do anything about it.

Out of the depths
of the stanza tragedy,
I cried for my body.

Wanderers, servants, maids, slaves, baristas, singing
with the dust cough, singing into the signing of books,
caught in the middle of the Great Pacific Garbage Patch,
Ivanka Trump's blonde hair swishes in this gyre.
We were banned through small administrative steps—
Cookie woke up from her AIDS death, my colleague laughed,
"the scene where Cookie is at the Catholic Church and pulls a rosary
out of Divine's ass," things would need to get so bad
before the uprising, I have to write poems for people
so I can remember what this human thing is, but even
then, the protests might not amount to anything.

Louis, I drove around aimlessly to find you, the four
days without my children crushed the sun and I meditated
on one card (the Fool), read the warning from the university
that said I couldn't teach the books I was teaching,
"The clitoris is too sexual," and "Why did you bring your kids
to the protest?" The police at the back
of the gathering. "Move faster! The problems we've had with
    the police
happen when people are outside the group." Lacey says,
    "Move forward!"
Regina in her orange vest, twenty-three years old, children
chanting, one little girl on the shoulders of her dad,
my kids' small legs moving faster than the adults,
everyone knows they kick the poets out first,
climate change deniers, and Chris's love in the pew,
I remember you, what you said spoke to me, the idea
of sanctuary, I am not religious, but I have been
broken, Lord, I have been broken
and, thus, am allowed to speak for the dead.

6

Feel the pain that grows
out like a nettle
from injustice,
and take that thorn
out of your paw, little one,
and keep walking north
through the snow.

Look at the people we have on our side:
Walter Benjamin is on our side
Hannah Arendt is on our side
James Baldwin is on our side
Sandra, they are all dead
But they are on our side
The other people,
the capitalists, who do they have?
They don't have anyone
All of their ideas are shit
Listen, we have Brecht
I was going crazy
I picked up my phone
I was talking to Maged

      Utopia   Utopia
    Utopia   Utopia
Utopia   Utopia

Maged is moving from Seattle
to Atlanta to be closer to his son

I dream of the New Jerusalem of love,
an Eden of sparks from the mouth of the rose cult

The rooster of Midtown cockadoodledoos,
crest shivers Floridian, last bit of cold
in these parts; I am the bold-hearted one.
Tallahassee on the "Dead Mall" Wiki page,
stock market up, earth crash, crypto-mining
the numeral seven like the delight of the godhead.
I smoke and ask my neighbor what he would do
if the government had him on a list of dissidents.

Demon of the windstorm, demon of talons and beaks,
I know you hear everything I sing, two children
huddled together, under the moon,
baby falling from a chariot of wildly shaped light.
What do we make of him? Wander the earth
in search of your brother. Brother, what would you do?
And something stupid takes over him,
"Well we are all on a list anyway," as he backslides
into his drunkenness, restoration of the neo-Nazi's
Twitter account and a 2:00 p.m. consciousness-raising
session, I wish I was high instead of inside
my body dragging itself to another action.

First National Women's Liberation meeting
in Tallahassee, but now I'm drunk, high, and smoking
a ton of cigarettes with my neighbor, the one
who saved me from Hurricane Whatever's 3:00 a.m. rainwater
pouring through the wolf-eyed tree holes of the ceiling—
then a MRSA infection on my elbow. No one knows

why a hurricane reddens the night sky, no one knows why
the ER doc says, "It's the dirty water.
It comes from farms, factories, collects
and then dumps down, so here is an IV antibiotic."

Sat in the ER, cried, but called no one,
emotions intensified like a Sabbath.
The handsome nurse talked
about surfing in Costa Rica while
my blood disinfected and outside
the hospital a Ouija board of plants
made a foreign language out of the night.

Man in neon coat walks uphill through the crows.
Reddish glow of the hurricane horizon
creeping toward the heart. Oldest woman
at the meeting talks about 1960 and '61.
"We were organized, we had an action.
They told us what to do and we did it,
then we'd go to jail and it was on to the next
action." Woke up—eyes puffy as windmills.
Thought of Rotterdam. That fucking poet
who didn't ask if he could hold my hand,
just grabbed it on the teeth chattering bridge
and then yelled, "We are poets! We are here!"
right into the river. And we walked into the spaceship
I mean hotel and in my room, I ordered
a panini and ate it on the white sheets, crumbs
on the white sheets. Mirrors everywhere.
Rotterdam, the last place I ever felt sexy.

I rise before everyone, kids at their dad's.
No commotion, rivers of clearing
eucalyptus mist in the aura factory
like pictures of Norway, her glaciated
remove languishes in a think tank
of food security, to want that kind of coldness,
to be surrounded by a swarm of bears
or love affair so north of here, but the winds
were shoved into the stone mouths of lions,
their rhymes tourniquets of counterfeit ideas.
And Rotterdam standing like an inquisition
of ships sloshing the metallic waters.

See, the thing is, Poet, you're failing.
You're failing at capitalism.
You're failing at "self-care."
You're failing at feminism.
You're failing at activism.
You've fallen deep into your addiction.
Your despair spreads everywhere.
None of this is your fault
but it's still happening.
The failure is the fracture is the opening
like that infection that started in your elbow
and moved to the depths of your being.
So maybe you should jump into it.
You spend the night reading about a god
cleaved in two so the dream demons come true.
Capitalism is shrinking and the rich
have gotten more violent. Capitalism could fail
and win at the same time.
Poet, this is called "crisis."
The swans and the trees and the birds are buzzing.
They don't care.
They hum.
Capitalism won.
I went on a run.
I am dumb I hum on my long run.

A series of demons dressed as birches
        tripping on the waterline of the riot.
The leaves and birds of the riot.
        The twigs of the riot
dispersed as demons disbanded
        to the center of the horned wreath.
A quickening like dust or lost resources.
            Some red dirt cries for Ra.
The resilient ones rise and fall
        as categories of storm light,
        as instruments of the godhead
spoken in a spiked language.
        Crowds flee their emblems at dusk.
        Away with her
        Away with him
In the morning you see someone
        stretching against the Gulf of Mexico.
The graves are the faces of striated flowers.
        The musculature of the urban landscape
ribbons like some vague concept of gasoline.

        In the morning, you are in love.

The material and its shadows unify
        to doves. Everything you doubted falls softly
            into an aubade of rainwater collected
        by strange and singular animals
                that roam the toxic dump.
You sing into a grave because it is there and apparent.
Maybe it is a window or the wooden frame
        of time crisscrossing the seas.

There are still purple ships and people still board them.
    You pick up a green comb
        and comb through your long, wicked hair.
            The coffee is good here. It is good here.

—⪤⪥—

To scroll past the body of the dead baby,
the baby that looks like a form of dust,
the baby of the desert is the baby of the sea
and the atrocities are piling up like hyperventilation.
They will build cities for themselves
and contain portraits of themselves
in the gemstones of their terrible philosophies.
They will be whimsical about genocide
and the pride they will feel in this volition
is like a brand of coffee or cereal
(nothing more or less).

I ran so far into the greenery that I saw
the purple rose that once grew in the blood
of the love garden, I saw the Jericho
of my tombs disseminate like the neurotic
spectacle of rainwater and then I vomited
like the queasy tides of history not
on our side and felt guilty and told no one.

The managerial class will punish us
with their monotonous, grueling blue eyes.
They will paw at our gates
and the houses will split open
as they go further in their quest
to forge digits, hemorrhage data.
Their constituents concentrate
on numerals as if their codes
were constructed by nuns.
Their unfailing power turns on itself
like love poems of pure possession,
like troubadour fantasies they tie
weights to your body and push you
gently into the blood river.
The factories in the background
are only imagined. They pump
and huff to transfix mimesis
like the face transplants of memes.
Flocks and flocks of stars
constellate the barbed wire
borders of the nation state.

—⅍←

This is where they plant cheap pine.
These kinds of trees don't communicate with each other.
This is not the ecology of the forest,
it's the ecology of a tree farm.
They create and destroy themselves for us
with no tie to the future or the past.

They used to make turpentine here.
A lot of workers tortured
in the convict leasing programs.
The company store was the only place to buy anything.
You worked all day in the swamp,
then you got yellow fever and died.

Rollover hedges all the way to the horizon.
I flipped through the pages of the Star Wars Journal
I bought my son. All the pages blank.
This is not a dystopia, it's wreckage.

"Should I bleach my hair today and shave part of it off?"
"I don't think so."
"Why not? I need a look as drastic as the world we live in."
The Garden of Eden in sculpted information.
"My love, your hair is long, wild, and beautiful."

Speculative cobwebs embroidered with flowers.
Back in the love garden of eternal truth, I am
as unhurried
as the smallest
creature left
to revel in its own zigzag.

Take the fucking wine away! Its red center,
the Saturns of my splendor and my emotional
landscape is cured for a day or a daydream is turned
into the vicious news cycle reeling in pain.

Destroy my body, take away the wine and the drugs
and the centers of my thinking
so naked before you.
Take away the music and the car and the job,
take away my body
and, once and for all, fuck riddles.

There is nothing mysterious to do here:
I am just goose bumps and nipples.

That hail is rare in South Georgia

That once my colleague saw a twelve-foot alligator on 319 before
they divided the road

That that was twenty years ago

That I regret reading an article on what it is *really* like to have
Trump-supporting parents

That I feel bad for saying that

That my kids are eating toast for breakfast this morning

That when they don't eat what I think they are supposed to eat,
the guilt is overwhelming

That I am a single mother

That my kids are age four and age seven

That maybe I should not have taught a four-year-old to use the
oven

That I hate soccer practice because I hate the other parents

That I tried to read Brecht at soccer practice but I felt like a snob

That the translation of Brecht was bad anyway and basically
unreadable

That I was cold and sick and the bench was cold and I didn't want
to touch the baby that someone brought to the practice and
said, "I don't want to touch your baby"

because I didn't want to get the baby sick

but maybe I just didn't feel like touching a baby

That it's probably communism or nothing

That fascism really kills your sex drive

That the rich don't need us all anymore

That *oh yeah* they never did need us all so what's the point of
writing this?

That maybe one time they did but that time is over

That probably they never did

That I already said that

That popular uprising may lead to nothing

That things that look like a "win" are often the very things that
pull us closer to loss

That popular uprising will probably lead to nothing or the
consolidation of the one percent's power

That it is unpopular to say this since it is not "positive"

That I had to convince my boyfriend that the one percent needs
to die

That he said can we not talk about murder before we go to sleep

That there needs to be a theory

That no theory is still a theory, just a bad one

That my four-year-old daughter is singing "Manic Monday" on
the way to preschool

That leaves are falling in South Georgia and it is beautiful in the
way that my daughter's singing is beautiful and this is the way
that some things, which are held together so precariously, are
also beautiful

      Daymoon, Utopia

That you came to me in those dreams and I tried not to be afraid
of you

That the dreams were never about the world falling apart as so
many dreamed

That this is not the apocalypse and we both know this

That someone will ask who the "you" of the poem is seriously
leave me alone

That I wish it was Sunday

That I wish it wasn't Monday

That it is Sunday and the leaves keep falling in South Georgia
across the field of nothing ever happens except for leaves
falling

That last week a hawk stared at me and I said, "What are you
looking at, hawk?" and it wouldn't fly away

That it came closer and closer to me

That a bird approaching a human is one of the most startling
   things in the world

That these creatures are generally scared of you

That the bird was not afraid of me or anyone or anything

That a friend posted the advice that if you feel lonely you should
   build a community but fuck community, I want my loneliness
   back since I deserve it

That Selena Gomez might or might not have gone to rehab for a
   cell phone addiction

That I would love for someone to feed me fruit in the desert for
   ninety days like I was Jesus or some other ornate martyr

That I drink too much or too little depending on the voltage

That sometimes people send me checks of money and I cash
   them immediately

That my boyfriend bought tickets to the opera is that what they
   call it?

That all operas end badly for women like screaming and
   breaking dishes

That I have often thought about operatic suicides and ordinary
   suicides like factories

That my language is something between an opera and a factory

That I might be bourgeois like commuting and soccer moms

That I feel like I'll never be a good enough leftist why am I not
   good enough for you?

That I have lived somewhere between an opera and a factory
   my entire life and that is called the moon on a windy night in
   South Georgia

That there are always animals in my dreams

That the nature of the future hides in the dreams of language
   like animals

That today I thought about the way the landlord is the boss is the
   president as I took a broom and gently swept a gecko to the
   front door of my apartment

Tallahassee. Tallahassee. Tallahassee.
Your mist today is incredible
as it settles on this rose garden!
When the largest rose shook off its dew
and looked at me like a cartoon, I smiled back
and promised not to break its neck.
And here we are together again, walking in a park
that honors dead children. A tree planted for each child
on such a mild day in December. And how the dead
children stream through me, scrolls of them:

Lily! Rose! Bobby!

Kierkegaard says anyone who follows through
on an idea becomes unpopular. And also
that a person needs a system, otherwise you
become mere personality. I need a system.
I need a
system. I need a system.
He must not have known
very many poets, so prone to tyrannical
shifts in mood. Change in weather equal to
don't let me go crazy. In the car on the way
to school Charlotte says, "I like to be gentle
with nature because I like nature."

But my mind won't rest, system-less,
as I drive like dread:

Lily! Rose! Bobby!

You're dead, you're dead.

The madness set in   as coral reefs bleached
This debt in my hands   will you take the rings?
One word would set me off   into the dust murmurs
of my own soul   rains barreling down   a lifetime of traumas
"I may not get better,"   I told you   nature is violent and I am too
What badness of men   miserable data-driven men   at the computer
was never going to solve   our strings   simple as corrugated dream
Nothing practical   in my iambs or slang   will save me from
the unnerving 666   Can you handle this?
Give me vitamins! Give me some   old operatic feelings
like the long sequestered   loves I have shot through my chest!

Inside   encrypted eternity   robots store my rosy data
They say I have   healing powers   and this morning   like a wave
I hail the glory of the jolie   Irish Elk   depicted in the nineteenth
century   lithograph   Oh kiss me   This is why I don't   believe in hell
other than a theory   of Iceland   I made up   in my bathtub
which involves   the middle   and upper classes   on vacation where
they don't have   to see or feel   this lush CO_2 overgrowth   the die offs

Goodbye, long-spined sea urchin   washed up   in that glossy red tide
I'm on a tour   of the magenta volcano   that blows   money and ash
the surface ice-slick   with debt   and credit in this epic
an industry   springs up   around the poet   who has not been able to read
quietly in years I confess   I wanted things   to be perfectly acute
and in that chrysalis   like nuclear energy   these worlds shoved
into containers   always exploded   blood from the mouth and nose

I owe the library my sorcery   Return the *Egyptian   Book of the Dead*
but I cannot eat   my abominations   under these palm trees
Happy is the corpse   that the rain   rains on!   How these fronds
are so bewitching   Gregorian chants   so bewitching
Autumn comes despite   monophonic grief   on a boat
which also carries   red grains of beer   Hail, guardian of the door!
I have made   my offering   Now, give us peace

The little gothic market
across the street
from this balcony
where the ice slopes
over the valley
and the afterschool
teenagers' shrieks cleave
leaves from trees
Oh my mind walked up
to the one with the orange
tennis racket in her lovely
hand and maybe she
was a he who then got
in the backseat
of a sea-green Volvo
and I said to no one, to the glassy
nothingness of the afternoon,
I just want to make you
something beautiful
enough that you forgive
me for being me
and they drove
off like the stateliness
of a midwinter parade

I'm so angry I will
    throw my fathers into
the supremacy of their
    wilted sacrament.
I'm so angry I will dance
    the love dance of roaches.
I'm so angry every cell
    in my body is a shard
        from the broken
    heart of a porcelain doll.

My skin, the Fahrenheit
    of my existence, burns
    Pollyannaish and strange.
Like an exorcism, I heave
    the gaudy flesh of my awakening
        and cut from existence
            my old selves
        as the moon twists the elms.
        My face, with its
        weakness for beauty,
        is the warped mask of purity.

Dear Jorge de Sena,

"I don't have enough money
to buy these books," is what you said in your book
in the bookstore in Princeton, New Jersey
        but I don't have enough
money to buy your book either
   so eventually I will put your book back
on the shelf but thank you.

Last week I read about a Putin
blown up by a million Erdoğans
in the Trump deluxe hotel complex
of biting sorrow, how I cried in the snow,
while my daughter sang "Let It Go,"

and now Jorge, I sit here reading your book,
punk-like and delighted,
scarfing down a Power Bar
that tastes like dust or lice or froth
bubbling from capitalism's labyrinth
while the clerics of money
sit in their divine tower
drinking Greek pine wine.

Jorge, before I go, answer me this.
Would you agree that half of the beauty
of the house of poetry is that it
never works out exactly?

(after Jack Spicer)

Dear Sandra,

I put letters in envelopes and receive magic in return. I, who wrote you in convoluted harmonics. Did you get any of them? Harmony is wine-shaped, the color of chords nocturnally bent and I am the flipside of that harmonic reckoning. Did you receive my letter about the drones killing migrants? When I don't hear from you, my paranoia grows like a great patch of ocean trash. The clouds today are syncopated.

No.
Poetry is not harmless.

You've asked before why I've had to take life to these drastic extremes. Maybe I'm drunk now. It is 3:00 a.m. and I've careened into something . . . how can I say? I hate myself sometimes. I hate my harmonic turns of phrase and my depression. Maybe I'm just dreaming of imaginary accolades that reach from the snowy little patches of my brain all the way out past those stark reservoirs and onward to Rome.

> Rome did not fall in a day.
> Neither does this.
> You won't either, Sandra.
> Sandra doesn't fall.
> She is not a ball gown.
> Nor does her double fall.
> Her double does not fall.

Yours,
Sandra

Psychedelic as thoughts of suicide,
the lamps hang low
on their blueberry branches
like another holiday.

I'm so sick of mortality!
(and the government).
I'm so sick of the destabilization
of self just to intensify the lyric
rushing with gold orbs and symphony.

Diet Coke and Skittles, I know you
don't mean to kill me,
so today I sing like a troubadour
synching up the centuries.

Oh fellow poets,
please don't steal
my little poems.

Instruments refract the social order
from trinket to libretto. You mistook
the clarinet for the flute, "This place is so tacky,"
the man said as the chandeliers rose at the Met.

LED lights extend across the stage,
make the ocean tip over while
troubadour poet, Jaufré Rudel, dreaming of death,
is stung by exactly one thousand and one bees.

I was instructed to walk a long way into the black
diamond forest: Go into the patch of poison ivy.
Place your hands over your face and kneel
into the lap of the earth   —and as I did this
the leaves   on the ground turned silver
and began to rise   all of them together

from their brittle deaths and I could hear their crackling
on the ground like the bones of a dog chasing a tennis ball
as the leaves turned the hours turned red
and the red fire turned white and the white
fire was my body and I held the white fire of my body
    for a little while
  and then the fire became a little girl
    and I brushed the little girl's hair
    and she fell asleep like a baby.

———————

          Sir, my poems are expensive; they cost me my life.
          My friends have all died this way too.
                    Infinitude, infinitude.

31

I stand in the middle of the Library of Congress.
      I am a tomb. The plainclothes
      police officer unties the soft ribbon
      from around my neck.
          "Off with her head!"

When nuclear energy mixes with the penis and money,
      one can't help but see design as a mass murderer.
Then, I found a clairvoyant note on the library floor:
    "Young man, my pussy is not the way to my genius."

It's going to hurt
You know this
So you drink tea in the morning instead
of an entire carafe of coffee

Like a vampire, your skin cells burn
on their first sip of the sun
The ringing taste of green tea or whatever
the fuck kind of tea this is

Describe to me in detail this so-called purification ritual
I can't
I've never done it before
My cells are exploding into a wasting lament
This is the last time you will ever write
yourself through this
On the other side of this swamp of dark water, a plane will crash
The lone survivor will speak on the radio
as you drive down Highway 27

In the middle of Florida in the middle of the night after you
step off the plane you see the swamps morph
into the mountains of your childhood
They raise their heads like giants
The Sierras stare; do not go there

"Brave soul," says the radio
"Beauty," says the radio
"It had to be like this," says the radio
"Difficult," says the radio
"Now you're forty-four years old?" says the radio
"That's right. Forty-four years old," says the radio

Continue to drive through hornets and testicular small towns
Some flags raised
Some flags down
The god of the underworld has let you go from his hand
into the empire Floridian
He says you have a pure heart
So pure he cannot destroy it
Some people look pure but they are not

He says he cannot see you destroy yourself so he has let you go
and he will protect you with his anger and melancholy

It will hurt
You know this

All the substances have got to go
Substances don't flow from your body
They leave with the violence
of an exorcism
Spicer says once a ghost leaves your body,
it never returns

"Horrendous," your sister texts
"I've been vomiting all night," she texts
"Maybe it will be a Christmas baby," you say
Something with no substance surrounds you

Dear Jack Spicer,

How late do you think that the grocery store will be open today? It's Christmas Eve. My refrigerator is empty and so is the world. This heavenly pain, what is it? A stigmata? And if so, whose? And if we find out whose, who do we give it back to? When I woke up, I wasn't sure I would live another day. There was a scratch down the side of my face and another one between my breasts. I mean, you can kill yourself accidentally. I know this. Despite myself, I check Donald Trump's Twitter. Is the word "minister" in "administration"? Probably not. I'm a bad speller. Measure me not by my actions, or the things I did when in despair. If nuclear war is here, "I do not know what it is like to have a chemical dependency."

I'm writing this from Miami.

Yours truly,
Sandra

Vision of Baudelaire   in this North Florida forest   looking into the eye
of a lizard with green   purple eyeliner zigzagging its way up a burnt log
Florida yew, olive, neon orange   day moon mushrooms
over the white bluffs   of the psychiatric Apalachicola River

Valéry says shells, flowers and crystals   are the privileged
objects of nature   harmonic underbelly,
endless, alien recycle   of gorge and interlude

George Michael died today   *For I live in a bubble of joy*
Go out into the sun!   the doctor says   your bloodwork
is totally normal   except for a   vitamin D deficiency
and left the office behind   and unleashed my sentimentality

A new obsession. How to get out
of the cold, metallic waters alive.
Every night for a week I dream
of my car ending up in a body
of water. If I'm not driving, someone
else is. Bob, the neighbor.
My new paranoia.
I google how to escape a car
filling with water. I watch videos
on YouTube. I memorize the steps
of what to do if this happens. First,
you take your seatbelt off. Late at night,
I read pages and pages on the internet.
What if the car lands
in the water flipped over?
Remember to stay calm.
If you panic, you will die.
News story about a woman who drives
her minivan into the ocean on purpose.
People on the beach run towards the water.
The two kids are strapped in the backseat.
One of the kids is screaming "No, mommy!"
What about the sunroof?
What if you land in the water
and your car has a sunroof?
My new car has a sunroof.
You have to let the car fill with water
so that pressure is equalized on both sides.
This is elementary physics.
If you don't do this, it's
impossible to open the doors.

This is the scary part.
You have to hold your breath.
None of the YouTube videos say anything
about what to do if you have
kids strapped in car seats in the back.
I look up what the dreams mean.
Water in dreams signifies turbulent emotions.
If you are in your car and there
is a flash flood, you should get out immediately.
Even six inches of water can sweep your car away.
Sweep it to where?
Maybe the forest?

I get nervous driving by the Gulf of Mexico.
My friend Dyan got into an accident
there and she said that if the car had
flipped on the other side of the road,
her whole family would
have ended up in the water.
I don't like water.
I don't want to touch it.
It scares me.
I know all life was born of water.
Today the government proposed
to sell off all public lands.
That before anything existed
there were rocks and then water.
I know that water is beautiful and mysterious.
But why does it sweep people away?
I want to push down the rising seas.
I look at a map of cities that will be underwater by 2100, 2200—
Jacksonville, New Orleans, Amsterdam.
I want to push them down with my bare hands.

In Shalimar, Florida, at night, inside the doom palms,
in the Korea House, we ordered boxes
of meat, the wind and the mermaids inside the snow,
so prismatic, I was the hourglass aglow and bikini
and you drank a beer, pure like crystallography.
We drove down Hollywood Blvd.
and laughed at the face of deterioration,
the all-American *Hotel Florida*,
the fire ants at our feet.
You said please write me a love poem.
My love, I shall do as you please:

I'm scared, Johannesburg
I'm scared, Jakarta
I'm scared, Dublin
I'm scared, Moscow
I'm scared, Jerusalem
I'm scared, Sydney
I'm scared, Nairobi
I'm scared, Helsinki
I'm scared, Marrakesh
I'm scared, Miami
I'm scared, Lima
I'm scared, Tokyo
I'm scared, Luanda
I'm scared, Shanghai
I'm scared, Kingston
I'm scared, Berlin
I'm scared, Detroit

Found a tulip-
shaped earring
at 30,000 feet
under my seat.
I had my headphones on.
The ones I bought at the Dollar Tree.
Only the left ear worked.
This is what I did when the world was dying:
Listened to shitty music.
I asked the people around me
if it was their earring.
I was listening to the Counting Crows
which is stupid.
We don't have the right vocabulary for anything.
If you actually knew
how I felt about myself deep down
you would probably cry. Yeah that's me
Princess Bonifay of the Country
of Lambs and Skeletons. Blame it on oblivion
that I'll drive back to Tallahassee
from Orlando through the terror swamps,
through the jabbering trailers and plastic gun
medallions and Florida rest stops where there
will be girls on the way back from driving
their lives into the ground and I will keep
thinking *did I leave my journal at your apartment?*
The passage where I said that I couldn't love
you anymore. I hope this airplane isn't broken
the way I am broken. "Too negative and dark."
"Is this your earring?"
"No." "No."   "No. Not my earring."

Tipsy on a seventeen-dollar glass of wine
bought at Newark airport.
A poet emailed me earlier today.
She said she was in Orlando
and thanked me for my poem "Orlando"
and that she might write a lyric essay
about Orlando and I was like that's cool
but is that your earring shaped like the pit
of my stomach or a musical instrument?

—pulled away from the internet absorption
to spare the plants—pulled away from
the plants to spare the kids, pulled away from the kids
to spare the poetry—pulled away from the poetry
to spare the grid. Read that the CIA
funded abstract expressionism.

—thought of Rothko—do you remember
that strand of hair we saw stuck in the orange
paint of his painting called "Highly Nervous,
He Continued to Smoke Incessantly"?
I click on a link called "death" always a first for thee.
One day in the museum—either in LA or some
other major metropolitan city. Then for ten
minutes, I allow myself to listen to the news
on the car radio, some reports of ICE officers
removing a woman with a brain tumor from
a Texas hospital—taught my kids
to walk to school. It's all
I can do; it's all I can do.

Spring proliferation of rain and cops.
National Weather Service alert.
What would they say if they knew I spent
all day making a cake shaped like a school
bus from a 1970s cookbook I found on a walk?
Passages of production. Touch them.

Sudden drop in the metallic temperature.
Today, I'm glad to be my salary.
Forget me not. There were so many services.
The Department of Homeland Security
SUV that trailed me from Tallahassee all
the way to South Georgia turned off
on a dirt road called Spring Hill.
No way to know which hyper-
cosmic abyss they sucked on, spit up.
Fatal slope of magnolia blossoms
inside the controlled burns. I look up
from the abandoned Sunnyside
Convenience Center parking lot,
a burnt palm leans against a wooden
electricity pole and I'm a monk.
The drugstore here sold such cheap
elixirs once. I wish to spend my life sealed
off from these structures of surveillance.

The lion or a grafted tree
as a sign of fertility, I gazed upon the tenure
of my feed where fake news doubled
with espresso and the media
was like some sort of incantation:

We are all so famous now.
We are all so famous.
Death, you are ridiculous,
with your freakish body,
whoring yourself out like that.

Behind the Four Rivers Smokehouse,
no ecology is left, just this opiate
fantasy of mineral water and some random
page of the Blue Cross /
Blue Shield health insurance plan
blows across the seismic parking lot.
I bought some vintage postcards—
"Texas Wildflower Collection" beyond
the robins so mellow a feel the spring
leaves as if this is some medieval day so the fairies
will take me into the "ah" of their hurrah.
"The number of pretty postcards is growing
everyday." Not wasting these cards on any president!
Field of bluebonnets, mustards, pink phlox,
white poppy and yucca, no browser opened
to the Midwestern couple who died in the front
seat of a Mustang strung out then OD'd while
their kids sat terrified in the backseat,
not enough says the death chime, but into
these night climes I ache happy for spring
has sprung even from this toxicity, even if earth
in full decline says poppy Oh, I also
saw a kit that teaches you how
to play the harmonica and such
mysterious strings exist inside the ear
light streams perfectly from some
alien space, I had to fix my technological
brain from that plunder, see the source
of kudzu sway March's wing, high on
the wind's grammar tree
"Wish you were in Texas with me."

"It was a beautiful spring day,"
which is how every horror story begins.
Then lightning struck the wing of my plane
and the light streaked into the hymn
forthcoming, a gothic hymn to jettison
by the River Jordan.

The next day, walked to CVS to buy
nail polish, body full of those spirits, bent over
the blush, had a nosebleed like in the movies
when everything's too much for the psychic,
utterly convinced some of the lightning
got stuck inside the cauldron of my head,
trying to get out of myself, I bled, I bled.

At the zoo today, the carnivalesque
vulture greets me. Hello, awkward
creature of our new century:
All eye. Mortality.
I think he likes my good looks.
I think he likes all the things
I know about death: *Oh you shall taste*
the sadness of my might
and be among my cloudy trophies hung.

The red bird falls from the tree, lands on
its head, rolls
right back up on its feet. Hello, spring.
Hello, sanity. Hello, trashfire century.
Hello, wilted leaves and gothic vines.
How are you doing?
I will water the thyme today.
I will make miniature succulents out of clay.
I will bake you the most beautiful loaf of bread,
eat half of it, and give the other half
to whatever nothing I can find, pretend
you are mine. How are you doing?

The stained glass of the ruined church
cuts through flesh like swords, then drive
to the cottages up the way, old bunk beds
made for children scattered inside ivy
and weeds. It is Easter. I knew they
beat them. But the kids must have also
slept and laughed and talked to each
other late at night. One of the boys drew
a palm tree and a sailboat
on the headboard. I touch the headboard.
When? In 1920? 1940? I take a picture
of it and put it on Instagram, then delete
the photo immediately. It's not right
to expose these raw wounds to the elements.
The ones who survived and told the story
of this school have an online support group.
They are getting so old. The next week
my friend Melanie texts me, the senate
has issued an official apology
to the Dozier survivors. "Maybe you
can interview one of them," she says.

"Everything is terrible."
When I opened the internet, these are the kinds
of things I would read. Then I looked away
from my computer and over at my kids:
the older one was teaching the younger
one how to set up the chessboard and they
were fighting over the queen. My little girl
couldn't sleep at night because she said
her friend Stella's dog died and the ghost of the dog
was barking at her all night. I said, "Charlotte,
dogs don't have ghosts," but what I meant was
dogs don't have to pull things together
the way we have to. Then I remembered
the sign at the zoo said, "*Shhhhhh*, the wolf
is pregnant so please be respectful," and I walked
her back to the bunk bed and tucked her in again.

Back at the zoo
my son and I walk the perimeter
of the "Garden of the Sun,"
which is what John Muir called Florida.
There was a certain generational inflection
to the phrase "everything is terrible"
which was hard for me to relate to.

With age, I began to understand something
about narration, that often we convince
ourselves we know where the story is going
and it's in fact the convinced part
we are up against.

My son and I walk past the sinkhole,
the reconstructed slave cabin.
"I'm the opposite of racist," my son declares,
"all my friends are black." My son
is eight and white and so we talk
about the structure,
structural racism, this structure,
that one, one cage, another, and another,
as we walk in circles, in a figure eight,
on the longleaf pine forest loop.

It's May. Don't you think the birds
of prey are loud today inside
this pretty hallucination anthology?
I dreamed I was filling out a form
called "The United States of America
Single Payer Health Care System."
The only place I wanted to be was outside—
wind's picking up. Nietzsche walked eight
hours a day. *The walking body has no identity.*
Who are you? I resigned myself
to the fact I would no longer
"heal from childhood trauma."
Child rape translated into . . . there would
be no way to chlorinate the truth.
Hello? Are you my future? Reader?

There was this bear cam
on the internet pointed at a place
called Brooks Falls, Alaska. A few years ago
my friend sent me a link to it.
I would watch it sometimes
but I never saw any bears.
Maybe it was bad luck
because my friend said she saw bears.
All I ever saw was the enormous river rushing
and the tall pines in the background doing nothing.
I mean that was okay, of course.
I loved the sound of the river
and wind in trees and the sheer thrill
that such a sublime nothingness
could be witnessed like this from so far away.

But I wanted to see a bear.
It seemed even more thrilling to be typing
in a cubicle and suddenly out of nowhere
there's a bear on your screen
that maybe fifty other people in the world catch
a glimpse of. Maybe they are on a break from Facebook
or filling out a spreadsheet and BOOM, a bear.

So, I thought while I was writing this
that I would just check the bear cam online
and sure enough a fat bear is in the middle of the river
eating a salmon right there in the Katmai National Park.
I get up from my desk and say, "You guys come here!"
and my colleagues come in my office but
by the time they run in the bear crosses the river,

or pixelated screen or whatever, salmon in his jaws
and the only thing there is the river
and trees and they say,
"Sandra, this is boring," and walk
back to their own offices.

Today, something about the Russians.
Today, I locked myself inside as my house grew hotter.
In the first month of summer, I ate some cheese like a rat
and smoked all my neighbor's cigarettes.
Today, something about Kissinger.
Today, something about gaslighting and damage.
Today, the spine is tired.
Today, I will do ballet until I don't have legs.
Today, I text Carmen about trauma.
Today, I will buy expensive bath bombs and bathe my misery away.
Today has to be more than damage.
Today, there is more damage and wreckage than wreckage alone.
Today, my body tells me there is only damage but that is unbelievable.
Carmen, this cannot be right.

Got off plane, dropped cell phone in parking lot
then someone drove right over it. The sky looked
like cellophane, filled with rain. First thought—
my hijacked neurons would give up.
Son asked me for a fidget spinner; I googled what
the hell that was. In flight, read a book on walking.
The walking body has no sense of time; it's like a staircase
with no entrance. It's like a staircase varying
the distance from no place to no place.
My hands shake into buying a drink
in the morning. I'm afraid of landing. The way writers
walk is various: Some stroll, some
try to escape, some wander, some avoid, some are
sentimental about the end of the world. My son
dreams of it. "Let's see what will happen
if I drive the remote control Batmobile off the bunk bed."

She steps into La Roue de Fortune movie theater
off the Jersey Turnpike, buys a ticket

and so swiftly the waters roll
above her instinctual visions: *Plaza, Il Piazzo*

creep of film over the sound of the words
Piano, Purr, whisper across her neck,

one door opens another
in the labyrinthine pitch to preserve

order, the expulsion from Eden, the dark
soda up her clear plastic straw, reels

of rodents, popcorn, teenage workers,
acne, blood and circulation turn to ice

inside this mechanized paradise,
where reality meets the sound of gardens

growing past their makers' dreams,
growing strange and outrageous.

She stops to check her phone
and the phone lights up *Putin, Botox,*

Trump, the garden grows outward, up,
to each side, the ghosts are simply

plants who forgot to stop growing;
they groan, shriek, quake, giggle, gurgle,

stare, and point fingers at the living.
I'm glad I'm in love, she thinks.

Last night, the wolf mother gave birth.
I could hear her howls and cries.
Good luck, Midnight.
Or maybe that was the wolf father
echoing through the zoo.
My neurons greet the new day.
Neuro-trans-meters low. Hurrah.
Read about subpoenas, indictments,
the stock market wavers slightly
like water around a stone, like deregulated
toxins in our streams. My son says,
"Mom, do you know how many steps
you have to take to burn one calorie?"
I don't know. "It takes one hundred steps," he says.
"In the first one hundred days, we are happy
to report we deregulated . . ." those silly
little things like streams. But they come
together, the watershed, the basin,
the aquifer, the small ones, hydrologically
speaking, we come together, my torn
calf muscle must be healing, one-minute run,
five-minute walk, then two-minute run,
and then seven-minute walk, no pain.
Nothing to white knuckle, I hear the wolf
mother again, wonder how many pups
she had last night under the royal palm.

After bath time, Charlotte and I watch
Mutual of Omaha's Wild Kingdom, a DVD
I got at the university library for free.
Ocher, shallow saturation, narrow spectrum
of pale green dawn trying to corral giraffes
into an area of savannah shaped like an arrow.
These grasses, birds—this was another earth.
My daughter puts her little feet up,
I read the Steele report on my phone.
"Put your phone down, Mommy."
I've never felt so unsexy. Is this what
it means to turn forty? I scroll through
the document wavy against the cracked
phone screen, the wardens of the park
say the giraffes will collapse the diamond-shaped
sky falls back down, it must be the early '80s on
this TV judging from these colors I didn't
know the world changes colors slightly
every decade the technology shifts
and hourly people type out codes to perform
a dance with your neurons these
antidepressants have gone kaput
and catapulted me into a news
obsession; the wolf mother
had four pups today, my daughter's
asleep now—I turn off everything.

"World events are not ruled by mercy,"
said Vladimir Lenin to his miniature
schnauzer one day while he made mint tea
in St. Petersburg. On TV, Turkish bodyguards
beat up peaceful DC protesters. I'm making
my daughter's cheese sandwich for school
and checking my son's math homework.
"A lie told often enough becomes the truth"
(Lenin really did say that, I looked it up). *Eight
times eight*   Montana GOP candidate
body slams reporter   *seven times seven*   Wake up,
the next day he wins. *Six times six* "A great victory!"
Five times five   I've lost too much weight
but the fleeing world won't hesitate. It's the last
day of the school year and we're going to Skate World.

What if one of the wolf pups dies?
What will I do? How will I hide
reality in my pelt so blue? Where will
I bring the feathers of the bird I killed
for you? Antidepressants, wine, treason,
the tattletale grows into the season.
I want to look good. Where do I buy
some mixed-blessing makeup?
Dumbed down or numbed down, it really
doesn't matter. Flabby thighs, loose skin,
brainstem dilemmas. The square root of the problem
shivers, I feel better; No, I'm under the weather.
Don't make me remember the long
and difficult division of labor.

A troll army from the Czech Republic
or a golden horse in Uzbekistan
full of the data of men and women.

A congressional letter demanding
transparency about the "Russian Laundromat"
scheme wherein money is suctioned

out of the proletariat's flesh sources,
siphoned, pumped, piped into Western
European currencies before the Bitcoin

soldiers were forged in the image
of Christ-like passwords, cues, fiddle music reminiscent
of nostalgia missions where long scripts are memorized

as their daily routines to inspect arms deals shoot across
the pilfered hills, bisected by the sonorous clouds, peppered
with corporate longing . . . . And a long time ago,

babies stolen, children raped, women abused,
pimps flourishing like flora, and concentrated this agony
into heavy points of extreme wealth. Amen.

The political necessity of cruelty
in its new authoritarian vision
working itself into the fabric
of our daily punch card bread.

A barbarous person
made fun of me . . . but, Sandra,
it was just a bot
and you responded to the media
projection of statecraft and guilt.

Three men shove families
into a raft to cross the Aegean.
　　The baby will die.
　　　So will the girl.
　　The mother-of-pearl waters
　　　with her blood red goats
　　will throw a bag of oranges
　　　into the sea and the entire
　　　story will be pulled to the bottom
　　anchored in capitalist trash.

Read of an ICE raid:
men, women and children sent
to a detention center
in Crawfordville, Florida.

Bought erasers, pencils and summer
workbooks for my children.

This is a cell.
All living things are made of cells.

This is the earth.
The earth is always changing.

The congressional caucus shovels
the national park's plants and rocks
into body bags and throws
those bags into the sea.

It is important to stay safe in science.
How do we stay safe?
Follow the rules and use the right tools.

Then a cooking class on YouTube.
The goddesses of Sunday welcome you.
We bring you this bowl of peaches
and serve you with our porcelain fingers.

Here is a napkin.
Here is a knife.

Your wife and children
are welcome too.

I like to photograph old signs
when I drive along the Emerald Coast.
"Florida Hotel: American Owned,"
"Rachel's Restaurant." I dreamed
a beautiful poem up by the sea but
forgot it by morning; Make America
Great Again vs Occupy Wall Street.
We talked about extreme weather
and the stock market in the Gulf,
the water fluctuating around the sun
and pelicans, text message alerts
for tornados and when I got home
I googled sinkholes and clicked on
the interactive map—fourteen by twelve feet,
eight by six, one by one, and read the warning
signs: maybe the doors to your house
don't close, maybe there are cracks
in the walls that grow or depressions
in your lawn; now imagine the bed
and furniture instantly falling into
the lawmaker's hand holding up a chunk
of limestone talking about an amendment
which will outlaw fracking in Florida,
"I've changed positions," she says, "Look
at this limestone. It's fragile. It's porous."
And wishing I remembered my dream squared
in the bulb of the sun, my body covered
by seawater, "It was almost as if
there were colored rings around
the sun," you said, and driving home,

the eye-level pelicans and their prehistoric
flight seemed calm, the bridge both flowing
into and forged by the breathless clouds.

Glandular fever punctuated by tropical storm Cindy which
was a dud; many weeks of rain, lymph nodes swollen, many weeks
of wind while the children played inside the supernova-like
    sinkhole.
Green tea and raw honey, our bees struggling for survival, Alex
searching for climate-controlled storage spaces, I yelled at
    everyone, the black
diamond and rattlesnake rattle fell upon me and I could tell you
    were trying
to communicate à la Ouija. I suspected it was your fault, seizure
    like substance
of air turned to current. Maybe I blamed you for my illness, I knew
you were the one taking me down through this amber realm,
this dream space, fragile, filled with neurons, jammed with signals
from the dead, then the realm spilled into the black hole of the
    summer
solstice and out of the storm, O Angel, you were born.

My friend made a song called, "Nikki, the Sun Is Out and I
Am Sick" to the sound of water dripping down the walls of
this satanic church, the blinds are drawn, the heat is a low,
orgasmic voice, the YouTube video in which a woman teaches
me how to make miniature succulents, cut out the tiny, mellow
leaves using colored polymer clays, Nikki, the sun is out and
the song is dusted with pigment from my eyes shoved through
the apex of my body as a man walks down the street carrying
the Seine under his blue and white umbrella, the low wail of
these church walls simmering, the maker's mind abandoned
in the pond, the koi fish, dead from exposure, their scales are
grins, and we all exist now in the darkest night of America and
forever we will stay here in America's terrible catacombs;

This song has no words, instead, it's a vision of a girl who slowly
turns her head around to stare at you and when she does, you
fly back against the church's walls dripping with blue liquid and
the only thing you feel is that you want to escape but you can't
because you are locked in that deepest part of the American
night like being sick and wanting to emerge from the flesh a
bird, wanting to emerge from scars as incantation but now
the song is the grave we stumble into and since the sun is out
and you are sick, you lie in the grave and you look at the sun
through this sick hole and there's nothing you can do because
you're immobile but the birds they fly past you and the cars
they drive by and the men who walk down the street carrying
black umbrellas continue to do so and Nikki, your body is
skinny and won't last, and my body is skinny and won't last and
even if we make love to each other, we are nothing against the
things that pass us, oh we are nothing against them.

The host "does not care for poetry,"
(twists and turns of the spectacle)
and will be moving from Los Angeles
to Alabama soon. They have a hall
of crosses made from toothpicks.
Har . . . har . . . har . . .
I document everything through the portholes
of my imagining. There was a time
when you did not love me, then you did,
then a time that you did not, shift to
Palos Verdes beach, "Will you watch
my things while I swim in the ocean?"
When the stranger returns, she mentions her
girlfriend, heir to the Maybelline fortune.
She seems nice enough until she talks
about the "undesirables" "invading"
the beach, my job is done, there's nothing
to discuss, I watch that woman
"of faith" (she talked about
that too) walk from the mansion
of the beach and sun, to the human mansion
of exploitation . . . . "O great sun."

—⚡←

What is Utopia? Is it heaven? Is it Utah?
Is it a ceremony?
Is it the place where your mother finally loves you?
Is it a place without sex slaves,

without goddesses or gods? Is it communism?
Is it drugs? Is it the best drugs?

Is it a hallucination of horses and steam in midwinter?
Is it the forest? Is it a little girl crying in the forest?

Is it never finding your way home?
Is it never flinching? Is it a gigantic hand
that will stop climate change?

Is it the end of government?
Is it longing?

Why do I long for you, anyway?

Is it a place without heartache
or is it the sweetness *of* heartache?

Why do we long for that constellation?
Why isn't this good enough?

Why isn't my body good enough
inside the atmosphere?
Is it a place without fear?

Are there gardens? Will you sing to me?

Are there credit scores and landlords there?
Will I live forever?

Will we always know each other?

Maybe we could write a ballad
together about the horizon's

purple color
sweeping across the throat.

Maybe it will
snow on the songs
we compose.

I asked my friend the point
of writing songs when it is obvious

there won't be a future to listen to them.
She asked me if I had eaten
anything today.

Do you know the difference between
a mere *Baby*

and a double *Baby Baby* and a triple *Baby Baby Baby*
and the ultimate

Baby, Baby, Baby, Baby
in a song?

Next time,
just keep listening for it.

Maybe the rich will build
compounds to keep us out

and maybe they will use technology
to keep themselves locked in, fed, housed.

Maybe they will chain themselves
to themselves as a Master chains

a dog to a metal post
as the dog runs round and round.

Healthcare gone
We're on our own

I watch videos
on how to live

off the grid
I don't know how

to live
on this grid
of the coinage

I could invent a stream
of knowledge
and inside my

dream we could
fish and swim

in the streams
of imaginative energy

and I could catch
the fish the way the landlord
collects the rent

and I could survive
off of my own
inventiveness

No trespassing: Private property!
I cross the line

"Look! Don't you see
the wild raspberries, Abraham?"

He takes a picture
of me beyond the human-

made limit and in the distance
I sense something cold
and bombed-out

mixed with the wild fruit.

—❊⟵

Write "ruin" Write "trauma" Write
"The dramatic logic of crisis"
Outline what you know in chalk
as one does the body at the crime scene
Then look at the sky welling up
Summarize I mean summon
how unusual it all was, how urgent

The war is armed with affect
so sensuous: candy thrown off the co-opted arsenal.
The army at the head of the army snakes
through the parade throwing
failure to the crowd. The war is armed
with hierarchy and discipline to hold high
corporatized wealth shaped like the head
of a snake at the head of the state.
General: many limbs sacrificed
at the expense of tender feelings.
Specific: Many limbs numb in order to create
the unification of body and spirit. This
might be called Romanticism.
The cohesion of the population glued
together with intense feeling.
This is the archaic torso of Apollo
unwound: so economic and visceral.
This is fascism's ripening fruit and we see
it in his marble eyes and lamp gaze
and because we are at the end
of inner experience, nothing can change it.

Our masters shift; this is the definition
of domination. Still, Esmeralda, if you would like
to take a dip in the filthy lake, I'm game
and if you still have the impulse to be mesmerized by love,
I'm down for that too.

I can even transform into a nude.
I'm a painting of paradise from the olden days.
It has horses in it and it's golden.
We could do this for a little while
before we have to go back to work again

inside the impenetrable flesh factory
where the meat screams
even though it is already dead.

Why does it scream night and day?
Maybe because it has no identity.

Esmeralda, they want our blood because
they must know how sunny it is,
how, long ago, we fed horses and wept and sang
by the fireplace; they must know

that we had such intense passions,
that we thought the grasshoppers
eating the yellow fields was beautiful
and we looked at both the creatures
and the fields with a kind of reverent awe.

Our passions
had to be held down
by a corresponding cruelty.
The formal laws of the state.
O the networks
of subjection are infinite.

The nonsense of plant life is a verdant push.
Summer's end redolent of energy,
remarkable as fresh cells   pounding out
the syllables   of the natural order of our axis
turned on its head like Morse code "I love yous"
in the crescendo of a rare eclipse.

What if I gamified my free time
capitalizing on the diamond
crux of the throat threaded in artificial
intelligence? A cat laps up the matrix
by the swimming pool where the old lady
talks sadly of Betsy
like a reminiscence and glimpses of momentary
fake frost over the great Floridian plains.

In dreams death   is not a passport   There's no   transportation
No River Styx   No coming or going   "No guide," I said
Not the light from   an open book   in a room of ancient libations
nor the marble-vaulted   Kropotkinskaia Metro Station   Not the architectur
of the vernacular   Not these preparations   for the apocalypse
Oh falcon-headed god   who guards the river   is that your tiny house
built on the   edge of the empire   with my ten-dollar donation to

St. Francis Wildlife Association   in exchange for eclipse glasses?   Permafros
thawing on the sun   Death is merely a body   cut in half by a machine:
sometimes a car   or factory wheel   sometimes a knife   or cult
But mostly it is the body   cut in half   by the eyes   There's so much
we don't know   Helen killed by a Nazi   in Charlottesville
on August 12, 2017   the day I turn forty   No blood in the spring
no blood on the shore   the eclipse brought on   my period

There was a wolf   at my door   then there were six
The protesters   were a wave   If ever birds   land on your shoulders
and you renounce   this mercantile life   the shadows elongated
the screen   hurt my eyes   On the bank stood   that lone
belted kingfisher   on the bank   of the vernacular   on the bank
of the flesh with a fish   glinting   in its beak
Please speak   like a piece of god

Permission slip signed   for kids to see   eclipse
Now let us   monetize our   agonized sensorium
Don't drain yourself today   of what you need
A sequence of scenes   Charlotte and I   on the beach
The beach is fake   made of salt   elderly people
line up to touch   the salt cliffs   with their naked
bodies as if   this was a shrine   Charlotte gets a sunburn

in minutes   passes out   hits her eye   it swells
she's still a toddler   a bunch of people gather around
a huge jewel   encrusted moth   flying in slow motion
by the cliff   the moth lands on   the hand of a woman
The sky fills with chickadees   each one weighs   eleven grams
People take their selfies   with the dream moth   alongside
the dream sea   and the dream beach   and the dream vermin

There is no future for us here   Who will read this?
This is not a climate   worth living in   I have brought children
into it   I have sacrificed nothing   There was not enough free time
to accomplish our   political goals   I go online to read an article
interpreting what the moth means   It is not good
I believe the interpretation   It's a scholarly paper
The chickadee   moth and child   disintegrate before me

Reader,
at what point
in the narrative
did you realize
you were deep
inside wreckage,
that you were
no longer
in the garden
amongst the trillium
and vines amongst the irises
and vines?
At what point
in the narrative
did you get up
to make some tea
and look at me
with those pissed-off eyes
and when I said
I cannot help you
you didn't know
what to make of it.
You thought you had called
a doctor
but it was just me,
The Hollows.
Knock knock.

1.
In the village, it rained continuously
for three years. It rained so much both the milk cartons
and children sprouted wings while seeds rotted in their
casings.
In the library of frozen shadows, golden light poured
through distinctive philosophical scores of the world
revealing the citizens' mechanized souls: notes
scattered like ants. A little girl in red cowboy boots
stood on a tortoise shell, the sea around her
smelled of cardamom and electricity until
the creation myth arced back on itself.

2.
I paged through some of the books
with Judy. "Beauty," Judy said, "is the spell
over the spell which devolves upon it."
"I dream too much," I told Judy.
"Beauty," Judy responded, "is that
which was once engulfed in dream."
You're not listening to me, I lamented
sitting on the square, red, velvet
pillow which was too small for my butt.

3.
Outside, the rain gave little shape
to the cultural history it dissolved.
The cops became swamps. The hashtags,
digital detritus, leading to broken reeds
in mud. A ghostly discussion about
malls, the fossils found beneath them,

half empty bottles of nail polish.
Canned goods gave us a
sinking feeling. "We tried," Judy
replied, and I couldn't tell if
she was a warm person.

4.
Everyone loves the light of the library,
how it spirals like that, how it connotes
Victorian miniatures, a frilly hat on its
skeletal hat rack, how it curls around
the throat, squeezing language, how
one might walk to the window and regard
the rain, not as an enemy or rival
but rather as a glimpse into the future,
the way a Ouija board might pull the fingers
toward an unexpected expression in the back
of the mind, like remembering the idea
there were one thousand days of analysis, yet no
synthesis of the system could be demonstrated,
not in diagrams, pictorial designs, not in
mimesis or tropes, not in the carnivalesque
characters such as Judy, myself
or the simple child standing on the tortoise shell
waving a silk handkerchief to the steamship
on the horizon of her youth, the light
that weaves its way into and out of
the library buoying itself against the rain
and it is windy now too so the long velvet curtains
sway from the inside out, carried by this wave,
and somehow we have managed to arrive here,
the bulk of us, confused passengers,
with so many friends and family
who could not be with us.

5.
We were studying for a third grade
test on the universe. I read the questions off
of the homework sheet. *What are stars? Does the sun*
revolve around the earth
or the earth around the sun? What is a galaxy?
What is the name of the galaxy we are in?
How many light years to Uranus?
Why does Uranus have a twenty-year-long summer?
Why are that planet's moons named
after characters in Shakespeare?

6.
I put the book back on the shelf
and it stopped raining and I had a lot of dishes to do.
I nagged my son about his test on the universe
and told my daughter to pack her bag
for dance lessons. The neighbor's cat
came over and drank water out of the toilet.
We were late for school. A student named
Judy texted me. I cursed the fact that I gave
her my number. "There's a quiz on
'The Fall of the House of Usher,'" I texted her.
I didn't want my kids to be late for school.
It was 7:55 a.m. I grabbed their lunchboxes,
stuffed them in their backpacks
and we drove off into another autumn.

ACKNOWLEDGMENTS

I would like to thank the following places for
publishing these poems.

Poetry Magazine
    When you think about it, mostly, a cage is air—
    It's going to hurt
    A new obsession. How to get out
    There was this bear cam
    She steps into La Roue de Fortune movie theater

Court Green
    Everyone dreams of the apocalypse, they are barfing
    Look at the people we have on our side
    The rooster of Midtown cockadoodledoos
    First National Women's Liberation meeting
    Man in neon coat walks uphill through the crows
    I rise before everyone, kids at their dad's
    "It was a beautiful spring day"

The Shallow Ends
    I am a terrible American

American Poetry Review
    See, the thing is, Poet, you're failing
    That hail is rare in South Georgia
    Tallahassee. Tallahassee. Tallahassee
    I'm so angry I will
    Dear Jorge de Sena
    "Everything is terrible"
    It's May. Don't you think the birds
    Today, something about the Russians

The Believer
   This is where they plant cheap pine

Poem-a-day on Poets.org
   Vision of Baudelaire in this North Florida forest looking into the eye
   (under the title, "The Garden of Eden")

Bennington Review
   In Shalimar, Florida, at night, inside the doom palms
   Found a tulip-
   —pulled away from the internet absorption

Lana Turner
   Behind the Four Rivers Smokehouse
   A troll army from the Czech Republic
   The political necessity of cruelty

The New Yorker
   The red bird falls from the tree, lands on
   (under the title, "April")

Boston Review: Poems for Political Disaster
   Wanderers, servants, maids, slaves, baristas, singing

Aquifer: The Florida Review Online
   I like to photograph old signs
   Our masters shift; this is the definition
   Read of an ICE raid
   Glandular fever punctuated by tropical storm Cindy which

The Brooklyn Rail
   Speculative cobwebs embroidered with flowers
   The madness set in as coral reefs bleached
   Spring proliferation of rain and cops
   Inside encrypted eternity robots store my rosy data

88

In dreams death is not a passport   There's no transportation
Permission slip signed for kids to see eclipse

New American Writing
    Last night, the wolf mother gave birth
    After bath time, Charlotte and I watch
    "World events are not ruled by mercy"
    What if one of the wolf pups dies?

The italicized lines in "At the zoo today, the carnivalesque" are from
John Keats' "Ode on Melancholy."

A few of the lines in my poem, "In the village, it rained continuously,"
are riffs on lines I found writing about John Ashbery's book *Girls on
the Run*. The poem was inspired by the writing of Janet Sarbanes and
is for her.

This book is for my past, present and future comrades.

INDEX OF FIRST LINES

ABOUT THE AUTHOR

Sandra Simonds has published six previous books of poetry: *Warsaw Bikini* (2009), *Mother Was a Tragic Girl* (2012), *The Sonnets* (2014), *Steal It Back* (2015), *Further Problems with Pleasure*, winner of the 2015 Akron Poetry Prize, and *Orlando* (2018). Her work was featured in *Best American Poetry* in 2014 and 2015, and has appeared in many literary journals, including *Poetry Magazine*, *American Poetry Review*, *Lana Turner*, *Chicago Review*, *Granta*, *Boston Review*, and *Court Green*. She is an associate professor of English and Humanities at Thomas University in Thomasville, Georgia, and she lives in Tallahassee, Florida.